Don't throw it away –
create something amazing!

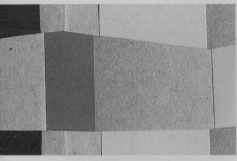

LONDON, NEW YORK, MUNICH,
MELBOURNE, AND DELHI

For **Stephen**

DESIGN • Jane Bull
EDITOR • Penelope Arlon
PHOTOGRAPHY • Andy Crawford
DESIGNER • Gemma Fletcher

PUBLISHING MANAGER • Sue Leonard
ART DIRECTOR • Rachael Foster
PRODUCTION EDITOR • Sean Daly

First published in Great Britain in 2008 by
Dorling Kindersley Limited
80 Strand, London WC2R 0RL

A Penguin Company

2 4 6 8 10 9 7 5 3 1
ND117 - 03/08

**A CIP catalogue record for this book
is available from the British Library**

ISBN: 978-1-4053-3161-6

Colour reproduction by MDP, UK
Printed and bound by Mohn Media, Germany

Are you
ready to
recycle?

**discover more at
www.dk.com**

Make it!

Here's what's in the book...

From trash to treasure 6-7

The 3 "Rs" to recycling 8-9

PAPER 10-27

Magic folds 12-13

Scrap-paper pots 14-15

How to make scrap pots 16-17

Junk-mail mâché 18-19

How to make mâché 20-21

Junk-mail jewels 22-23

Paper weaving 24-25

Paper portraits 26-27

PLASTIC 28-39

Rainbow frame 30-31

Bottle bank 32-33

Bottle-top art 34-35

Plastic party 36-37

Plastic wrappers 38-39

METAL 40-49

Mysterious metal 42-43

Metal muddle 44-45

Mirror mobiles 46-47

Metal models 48-49

FABRIC 50-63

Making friends 52-53

Hold onto your hats! 54-55

Rag mats 56-57

Pocket purses 58-59

How to make a glam bag 60-61

Comfy cushions 62-63

Index 63

From Trash...

Looking for materials? These come **FREE** to you every day – so don't dump valuable stuff. Use it to make something new – RECYCLE IT, and help the planet too!

Throw away?
NO WAY!

Did you know? Most of our rubbish gets buried in the ground...

...or burnt.

All this stuff costs money to make and costs the Earth too.

Don't throw me away. I'm **plastic** so I'll last a lifetime!

Don't fork out for new materials – you get me for FREE! USE ME AGAIN and again and again...

STARVE YOUR BIN
Recycle your stuff

If all this rubbish gets buried, it really will be **"buried treasure"**.

It's crazy! Don't bury rubbish. It doesn't go away!

6

...to TREASURE

Make
something
NEW

So DON'T TRASH it – TREASURE it!

The 3 "Rs" to recycling

It's not all rubbish – about half the stuff we throw in the bin can be recycled. Remember the three "Rs" and help to keep rubbish out of landfill sites and incinerators.

Why should you do the 3 "Rs"?

Watch how much rubbish your family throws out each week – it will surprise you. All that rubbish has to go somewhere and that somewhere is an incinerator where it is burned, or a landfill site where it is buried. A lot of what we put in landfill sites, such as plastic, will remain there for hundreds of years. There is a famous landfill in New York City called *Fresh Kills* that is now so big, it has become the largest man-made structure in the world.

What if you don't?

If we continue to throw away as much rubbish as we do now, landfill sites will get bigger and bigger, and burning rubbish causes air pollution and toxic ashes. We all need clean air and water to survive, and if we don't reduce, reuse, and recycle, we will damage our world. Help our planet be a healthy place to live, not just for you and me but for animals and plants as well.

Reduce

Means finding ways to cut down on rubbish. Don't accept plastic bags from shops – take your own bag.

Reuse

Means finding ways to use things again and again and again without throwing them away.

Close the circle
Try to buy more products made from recycled material to help to close the circle.

Recycle

Means taking something old and turning it into something new.

! Ask an ADULT
Watch out, you may need some help along the way in this book.

YOU can help

Here are ideas for things you can do to help.

- Buy items with little or no packaging. This will reduce your rubbish.

- Refill your drinks bottles and keep reusing them.

- Buy, sell, or donate your things. Don't throw them away – help a charity.

- Use both sides of a sheet of paper before recycling it.

- Get the family involved – recycling only works if everyone joins in.

- Find out about recycling in your area, then use your local bins.

Sort your stuff

In this book the materials are divided into four sections – paper, plastic, metal, and fabric.

Know your stuff

To help you understand why it's important to recycle materials, it helps to know some facts about them. Look out for the "Know your stuff" circles that appear in this book.

KNOW YOUR STUFF
Facts about a material. They appear throughout the book.

Get recycling

• Use different bins for each material.

• Some packaging is made of more than one material, so make sure you separate them before you recycle.

• Before you bin anything, make sure you can't reuse it first.

Paper

Newspapers
Wrapping paper
Magazines
Envelopes
Comics
Cardboard boxes
Cartons

Plastic

Drinks bottles
Straws
Bottle tops
Carrier bags
Toys

Metal

Foil wrap
Foil food trays
Drink cans
Food cans
Paperclips
Safety pins
Paper fasteners
Wire

Fabric

T-shirts
Cotton skirts
Denim jeans
Woolly socks and gloves
Nylon tights
Ribbon

Try recycling your paper to make these scrap pots.

Paper – the best invention in the world!

We paint on it, we read and write on it, we can fold it into shapes, we can wrap presents in it, and much, much more.

Paper

Imagine our world without paper – that would mean no letters, no cardboard packaging, no newspapers, no wrapping paper, and no toilet roll!

What is paper made from?

Most of the paper we use is made from trees. Billions of pine trees are cut down every year to make our paper.

When was paper invented?

Paper has been around for thousands of years. The ancient Egyptians made it from the papyrus plant. That's where we got the word paper.

How is paper made?

The trees are chopped up into little pieces called chips. They are then made into a mushy pulp and a lot of chemicals and water are added. The pulp is then rolled flat into paper.

Paper gets thrown away more than any other material.

Think about how many newspapers are made everyday that end up as rubbish.

Paper uses

We use paper all the time. Count how many times you come across paper in one day. You'll be surprised how much there is out there. Now imagine how many trees have been cut down to make it.

Look out for the symbol

Try to buy recycled paper – look for this symbol, you'll find it on anything from cartons and stationery to toilet rolls.

Recycled paper

Recycled paper contains fewer chemicals and bleaches than brand-new paper, and it saves trees too. A piece of paper can't be recycled forever, however, because the fibres will start to break down. High-grade paper can be remade into newspapers and magazines and these can go on to become egg cartons.

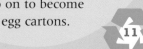

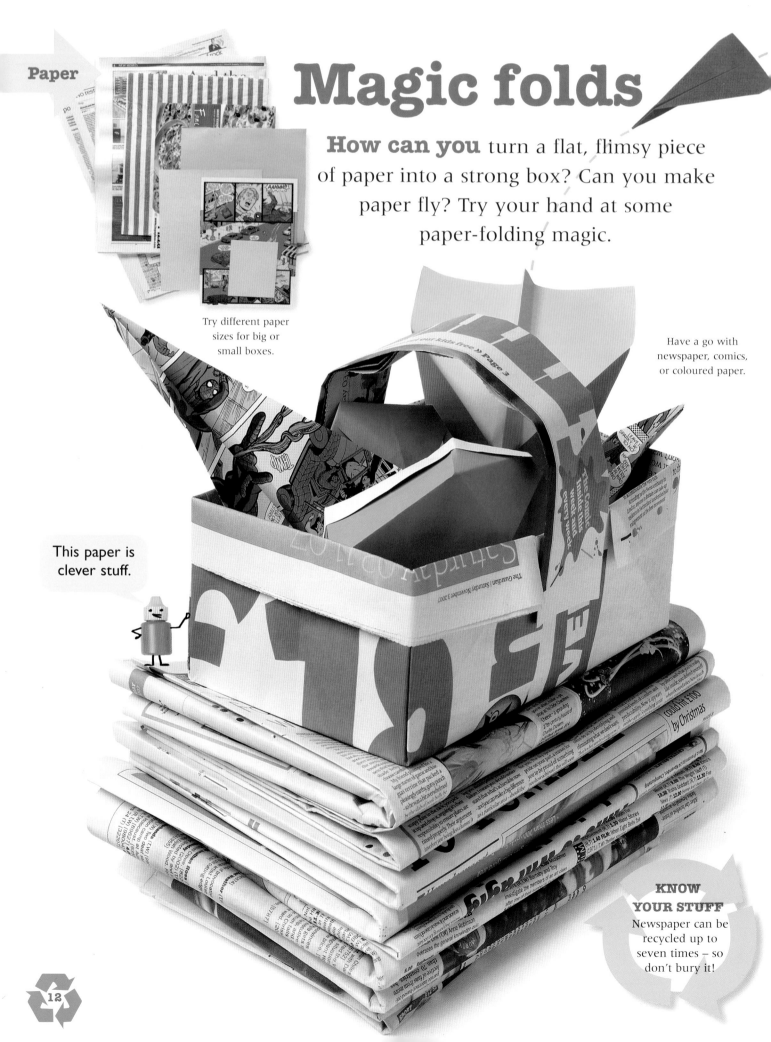

Magic folds

How can you turn a flat, flimsy piece of paper into a strong box? Can you make paper fly? Try your hand at some paper-folding magic.

Try different paper sizes for big or small boxes.

Have a go with newspaper, comics, or coloured paper.

This paper is clever stuff.

KNOW YOUR STUFF
Newspaper can be recycled up to seven times – so don't bury it!

Perform PAPER magic

Fold and hold – just a few folds and tucks and a flat piece of paper becomes a sturdy box. That's paper magic!

Fold a rectangle of paper in half and half again four times to make 16 squares. Then unfold it.

Bring the top and bottom flaps into the centre.

Fold each corner down two-thirds to the centre.

Fold up the two flaps so the corners are tucked in.

Hold the centre of the two sides and pull them apart.

Pinch each corner from top to bottom to help form the shape of the box.

Cut a wide strip of paper for a handle.

Staple the handle to each side.

Try using patterned paper or paint a piece yourself.

Watch paper fly!

Paper plane – a few simple folds and it flies!

Take a rectangle of paper and fold it in half.

Turn down one corner, as shown.

Fold the same corner down again.

Now fold the top part down to make a wing.

Now make the other wing

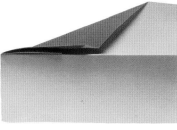

Repeat the folds on the other half of the paper.

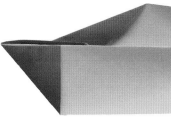

Open out the wings, turn the plane over, and whizz it across the room!

13

Pumpkin pot.

Scrap paper pots

Paper is everywhere.
Just think about how much
is thrown away each day.
Why not turn your scraps
into funky pots.

Look out for scraps of the same
colour for a solid look.

**Tree
frog pot...**

Magazine scraps
make colourful pots.

The frog pot is made
from lots of pictures of
trees from magazines.

**KNOW
YOUR STUFF**
Recycled magazines and
comics can be moulded
into paper products like
egg cartons.

14

The insides of envelopes make up this scrap pot......

Envelope pot

Sweet wrappers give this pot a shiny look......

Tissue pot......

Sweetie pot

Torn tissue paper gives a great ragged effect.......

Comic pot

Tear up favourite comic strips for a cartoon pot......

Home-made paste

This simple home-made paste works really well with your paper projects, and the good news is it's completely eco-friendly. Your projects can be recycled afterwards because the ingredients are natural. This paste works best fresh so make a new batch for each project.

You will need:

1 cup plain flour

3 cups water

! **Ask an ADULT**
to help heat up the saucepan.

1.

Put one cup of water and one cup of flour into a saucepan.

Stir with a wooden spoon until the mixture is smooth.

2.

Keep stirring!

Add the rest of the water and bring the mixture to the boil, stirring all the time. Then turn off the heat.

3.

Home-made paste

Pour into a bowl and allow to cool.

NOW IT'S READY TO USE!

Make a newspaper pot

Use your home-made paste. You will also need petroleum jelly, a plastic bowl, and lots of old torn-up newspaper. For your pot and lid, make two bowls, which you can decorate when they are dry.

Grease a bowl with petroleum jelly to stop the paper from sticking to it.

Tear up lots and lots of newspaper strips, about 2 x 4 cm (1 x 2 in).

1.

Place a layer of paper directly onto the greased bowl.

2.

Brush on a layer of paste.

3.

Add another layer of paper.

4.

Keep adding the paste and paper until you have about six layers.

5.

Leave the bowl to dry out completely.

6.

Remove the bowl and trim off the rough edge.

Decorate your scrap pots

When your two bowls are dry, start decorating. One bowl will be the base and the other will be the lid. Use the home-made paste to stick on any colourful strips of paper.

Paste the outside and inside.

Experiment with different types of paper.

Tear up pieces of coloured paper and cover your pot with them.

Tear out circles to make a frog face.

Paste them in place.

! Ask an ADULT to help you make a slit in the lid.

Make a tissue bowl

Make a tissue bowl the same way as the newspaper bowl – just use tissue paper instead.

Make a handle

To add a handle, ask an adult to make a slit in the lid. Cut out a strip of thick paper, about 7 x 2 cm (3 x 1 in), and fold it in the middle. Push it through the lid and tape it in place on the inside.

Leave to dry completely before removing the bowl.

Tear up pieces of tissue paper.

Grease the bowl.

Add a layer of tissue paper, then, using the paste, build up about 10–12 layers.

Junk-mail mâché

Envelopes

Fliers

Brown paper

Paper is delivered to your door every day – for free! Don't just chuck it, collect it up and make some junk-mail mâché.

Gift wrap

Adverts

Free Magazines

Magazines

Little bits of junk mail

KNOW YOUR STUFF
If you don't use your junk mail, make sure you recycle it.

Envelopes

Think before you throw away envelopes. Greetings cards come in all sorts of coloured ones.

Junk mail

Sort through your junk mail and keep the bright bits. Remember to recycle the rest!

Paper boy

Colour pots

Sort your scraps into colours and you can make single-colour pots.

Pots as presents

How to make junk-mail mâché

Tearing and mulching

The great thing about junk-mail mâché is that it gets really messy! So roll up your sleeves and get stuck in.

Start by tearing lots of paper into tiny pieces. You can sort them into colours or mix them up.

1.

Fill a plastic bowl with your paper pieces. Pour on hot water.

! Ask an ADULT for help with the hot water.

2.

Make sure the water covers the paper.

3.

Leave the paper for three hours. Then pour away the water through a sieve.

Squeeze the paper as dry as you can.

4.

Spoon some eco paste (see page 16) into your mixture, then mix it with your hands until it's a gluey mulch. Tear up the paper some more as you work.

How to make mâché bowls

Now it's time to spread the mulch around a plastic bowl. Do it bit by bit rather than putting the whole lot in at once.

Rub some petroleum jelly all over the inside of a plastic bowl. This will stop the mulch from sticking.

1.

2.

Press your mulch hard against the inside of the bowl.

3.

Don't worry if you leave holes here and there. This adds to the character!

4.

Leave it to dry overnight or until it is really hard and dry. Use a knife to loosen around the edge of the bowl carefully.

5.

Lift it out and fill it up with goodies!

Junk-mail jewels

Your junk-mail mâché can also be made into fantastic jewels.

Cookie-cutter shapes

Place a cookie cutter on a piece of plastic to stop it from sticking. Take a small amount of damp mâché and press it into the cutter. Push the shape out onto a sheet of kitchen towel. Then make a hole for some string, and leave to dry.

Cookie cutters

Press the mâché firmly inside the cookie shape.

Make the hole with a cocktail stick.

Push out onto the paper.

Paper towel

Piece of plastic

22

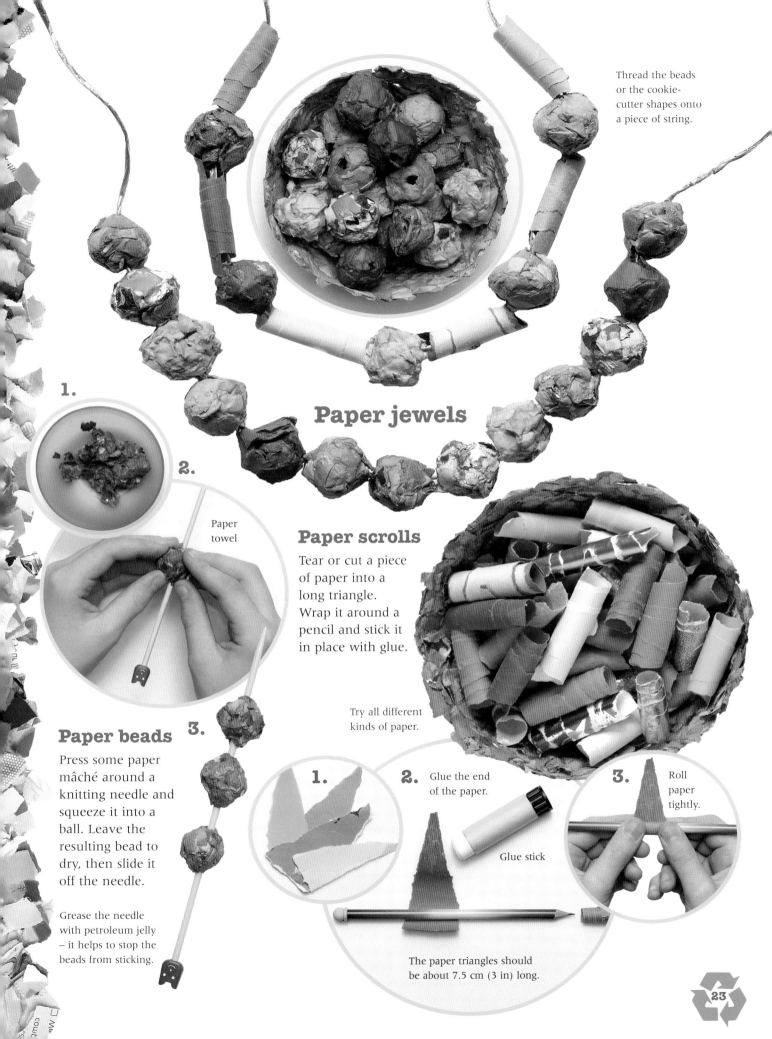

Thread the beads or the cookie-cutter shapes onto a piece of string.

Paper jewels

Paper scrolls

Tear or cut a piece of paper into a long triangle. Wrap it around a pencil and stick it in place with glue.

Try all different kinds of paper.

1.

2.

Paper towel

Paper beads

3.

Press some paper mâché around a knitting needle and squeeze it into a ball. Leave the resulting bead to dry, then slide it off the needle.

Grease the needle with petroleum jelly – it helps to stop the beads from sticking.

1.

2. Glue the end of the paper.

Glue stick

3. Roll paper tightly.

The paper triangles should be about 7.5 cm (3 in) long.

Paper weaving

Under, over, under, over. Don't throw paper away – turn it into art.
Weave pictures and turn them into cards, or stick them on the wall.

1. Take an envelope and cut along the short sides and one long side. Cut off the flap too.

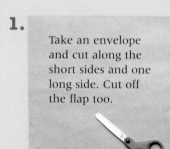

2. When you open it out you should have a large sheet of paper, like this.

3. Fold the paper in half again and draw evenly spaced lines down the sheet.

4. Cut the strips from the folded edge but STOP before you get to the top.

5. Open the sheet out. Under, over, under, over, until you get to the end. Remember to start the next strip in the opposite way – over, under, over, under.

Cut wiggly lines up the sheet for a wavy look.

KNOW YOUR STUFF

In a landfill site, a ton of paper fills the space that's about the size of a car – so recycle!

Cut lots of paper strips that fit across the width of the sheet.

24

Under, over, under, over, weave, weave, weave

Picture weave

Try using a picture from a magazine as your backing sheet, then weave plain strips along it.

Weave art

Experiment with your weaving by using pictures or patterns as well as plain paper. Use any paper you can find.

Try patterned strips and a plain background.

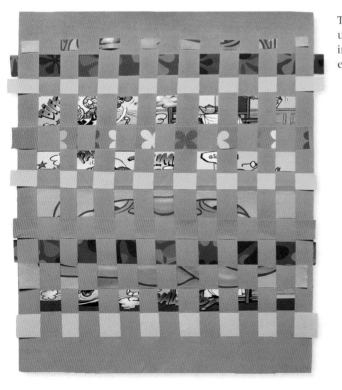

Turn your weaves into colourful cards.

This weave uses the inside of envelopes....

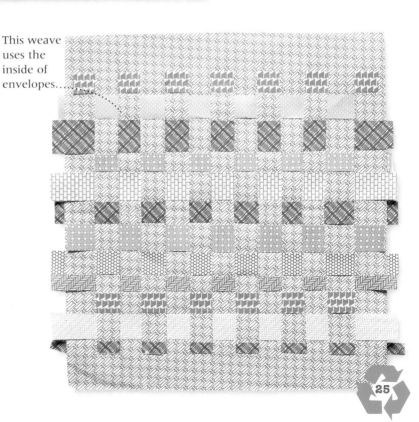

Paper portraits

Picture in a box

Turn old pictures into new ones – then frame them in a box.

KNOW YOUR STUFF
Recycling a 1 m (3 ft) stack of flattened boxes can SAVE ONE TREE.

Box frames

Stop your family from throwing away old food boxes.

You will need:

- A cereal box
- Lots of pictures, postcards, junk mail, and colourful patterns from old magazines.
.

Draw a line around the edge of the front of the box leaving a 2 cm (1 in) border. Then cut it out.

1.

Use the piece of card you cut out of the box as your picture.

Tear strips of blue paper as a sea background and glue them on. It doesn't have to look neat. Try different shades of blue for a stormy effect.

Glue stick

2. Glue scraps roughly for a 3-D effect.

Now cut or tear pieces of paper – keeping the shape of some objects, but tearing others roughly to create a textured edge.

Attach a few shapes using a card strip so they stand away from the picture and look three dimensional.

3.

When you have glued your picture, you may want to make a border around the edge with extra pieces of torn paper.

Slip your picture inside your box and glue it to the back.

Take a closer look — can you tell what the pictures used to be?

Blue towel

Chocolate hair

Carpet face

Car-bonnet shirt

Corn field

Rubber gloves

Grass

Number

Letters

Red towel

Coffee beans

Pizza

Apples

Let the tissue paper flap over for a wavy plant look.

27

Reuse your plastic bits and pieces and have yourself a plastic party!

Plastic – it's fantastic!

It can be shiny, smooth, rough, tough, hard or soft. It can be any colour, AND it can be moulded into any shape.

Plastic

Imagine our world without plastic – there would be no plastic toys, plastic packaging or plastic telephones. Plastic is easy to make BUT it's not so easy to get rid of.

What is plastic made from?

Like paper, plastic comes from trees. Some clever scientists got a substance called cellulose out of wood pulp and that made plastic.

When was it invented?

In 1862 a British chemist called Alexander Parkes was experimenting with cellulose. He heated it, moulded it, and found that when it cooled, it kept its shape. Plastic was born.

Plastic today

After pulping wood to get plastic, chemists started creating it in laboratories. They use chemicals to make plastics such as polythene and polystyrene.

Plastic problem

DID YOU KNOW?
If you lined up all the foam plastic cups made in a day, they would reach around the Earth.

Plastic uses

Take a look around your bedroom – I bet you can spot at least ten pieces of plastic. Perhaps you have a CD player – and what about all your pens and toy animals?

Look out for the symbols

Most plastic items you buy have a symbol on them. The PETE 1 symbol is the one to watch for.

Recycling plastic PETE 1

PETE 1 plastic, which is found in most drinks bottles, can be recycled easily. It can be turned into clothing, stuffing for sleeping bags, stuffed toys, rulers, and lots, lots more. So make sure you recycle all your water and soft-drinks bottles.

Rainbow frame

Plastic comes in so many great colours – so gather all those tiny plastic bits and pieces and make one of these fantastic plastic frames.

Now they look as pretty as a picture.

KNOW YOUR STUFF
Don't bury your plastic – it'll be there for hundreds of years.

1. Tidy your toys

Sort your plastic bits and bobs into rainbow colours.

Things look tidy already!

2.

Make a frame

Use card from an old cardboard box.

! Ask an ADULT to help cut out a frame shape.

3.

Cover it with all your plastic.

Glue the pieces in their colour groups.

Stick on the bits

Crazy ice

Cut the bottoms off plastic bottles, fill them with water, and freeze.

Colour the water with food colouring.

Refill Refill Refill

For picnics, refill bottles with your own home-made drinks.

KNOW YOUR STUFF

Recycle your bottles – 12 of them can be turned into a new fleece top.

Skittle game

Set up 10 bottles and knock them down.

A ball of screwed-up paper will work too...

Bottle bank

Plastic bottles will last for hundreds of years, so it's crazy to use them only once. Here are some ways to reuse them.

Mini plant cover

Half a plastic bottle placed over your seedlings will keep them warm and help them grow.

Make the most of me!

! **Ask an ADULT** to help you cut the bottles. Plastic can be tough.

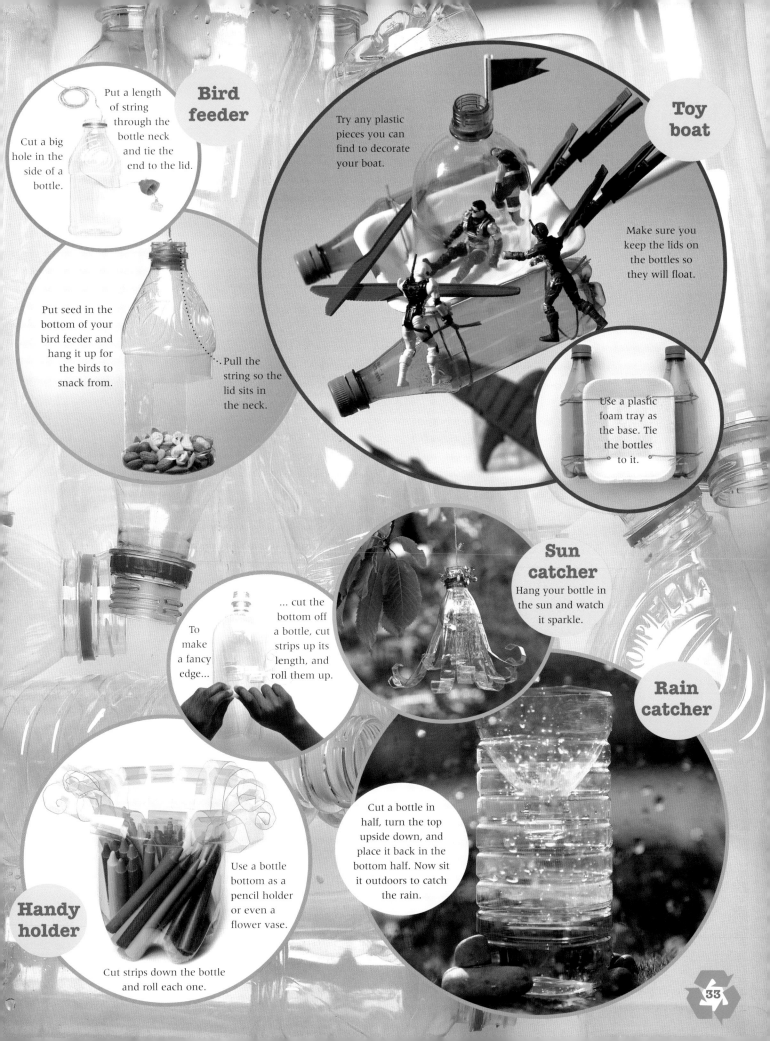

Bird feeder

Put a length of string through the bottle neck and tie the end to the lid.

Cut a big hole in the side of a bottle.

Put seed in the bottom of your bird feeder and hang it up for the birds to snack from.

Pull the string so the lid sits in the neck.

Toy boat

Try any plastic pieces you can find to decorate your boat.

Make sure you keep the lids on the bottles so they will float.

Use a plastic foam tray as the base. Tie the bottles to it.

Sun catcher

Hang your bottle in the sun and watch it sparkle.

To make a fancy edge... ... cut the bottom off a bottle, cut strips up its length, and roll them up.

Rain catcher

Cut a bottle in half, turn the top upside down, and place it back in the bottom half. Now sit it outdoors to catch the rain.

Handy holder

Use a bottle bottom as a pencil holder or even a flower vase.

Cut strips down the bottle and roll each one.

Bottle-top art

Lots of bottles means lots of lids. You'll be amazed how they mount up.

1. Use a plastic foam sheet, like a pizza base or foam packaging.

2. Start from the centre. Use strong glue to stick the tops to the base.

3. Keep adding to your pattern.

Careful – I could lose my head!

Bottle-top patterns

Collect lots of pretty coloured lids and make patterns with them. You can hang them on a wall or even use them as place mats or colourful coasters.

Try different designs

KNOW YOUR STUFF
TOPS OFF when you recycle your plastic bottles. The tops are made of a different plastic, which isn't as easy to recycle.

Bottle-top badges

Collect up your bottle tops and fill them with lots of tiny plastic beads, buttons, and toys.

Sticky labels

Make sure you clean the lids.

Safety pins ·····

1.　　**2.**　　**3.**

·····Attach a safety pin to the back of the badge using a sticky label.

Use strong glue to keep everything in place.

Try matching the colours so each badge has a theme. ·····

Tie and hang

Tie each end of
the streamers
securely so they
don't come undone,
then hang them up.

Who knew plastic
could be so
much fun!

Plastic party

Bottle banners and
pen-top streamers
brighten up any party.
And you don't have to
buy decorations at all –
just reuse and recycle!

What to use

Next time you are at a party, gather up
the used party popper bottles – they're
great for streamers. Keep an eye out for
pen and bottle lids, pegs, and straws too.

36

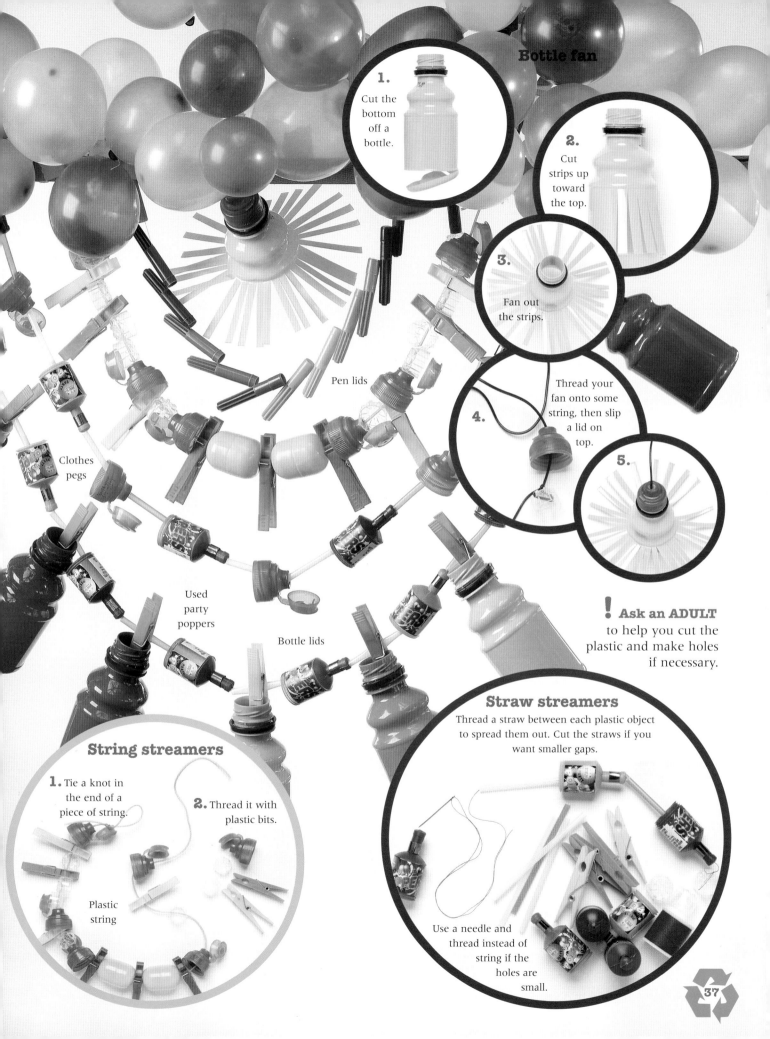

Bottle fan

1. Cut the bottom off a bottle.

2. Cut strips up toward the top.

3. Fan out the strips.

4. Thread your fan onto some string, then slip a lid on top.

5.

! **Ask an ADULT** to help you cut the plastic and make holes if necessary.

Pen lids

Clothes pegs

Used party poppers

Bottle lids

String streamers

1. Tie a knot in the end of a piece of string.

2. Thread it with plastic bits.

Plastic string

Straw streamers

Thread a straw between each plastic object to spread them out. Cut the straws if you want smaller gaps.

Use a needle and thread instead of string if the holes are small.

Plastic wrappers

Brighten up your room. Turn plastic wrappers into a colourful cushion or shiny screen.

Decide how big you want your cushion and cut a rectangle double that size out of bubble wrap.

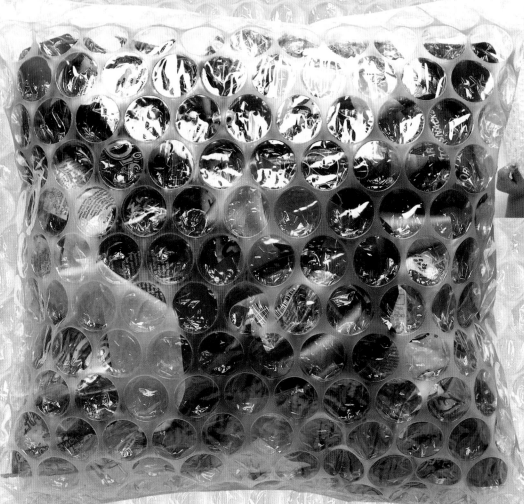

Fold the bubble wrap in half and tape up two of the open sides with sticky tape.

Stuff the bubble wrap

Bubble-wrap cushions are easy to make, but the real art is in the stuffing. Bubble wrap is see-through, so make sure you stuff it with lots of colourful plastic bits and pieces. When you have finished stuffing, tape up the open side.

This will make you comfortable.

KNOW YOUR STUFF

Sweet wrappers and crisp packets make up a huge proportion of what you throw away.

How to make a sweetie-wrap screen

Take a length of netting material and cut a pole to hang it from. Fold the top of the net over the pole and glue it down. Collect lots of plastic sweetie wrappers and buttons and get decorating.

Cut the pole long enough to poke out on each side of the net.

Use glue to stick the netting down and to attach the decorations.

Cellophane sweet wrappers

You can use an old net curtain for the screen, or the type of netting in a ballet tutu.

Nylon netting material

Plastic buttons

Wow, metal's amazing! It's in everything from paperclips to spaceships.

Metal – is magical!

It can be shiny and cold, strong, wiry, smooth, or sharp.
It's magnetic, can carry electricity, and it's valuable stuff too.

Metal

Imagine our world without metal – We wouldn't have any money, jewellery, or skyscraper buildings, and we would have a very difficult time cooking.

COPPER   TIN
ALUMINIUM
NICKEL   IRON

GOLD
SILVER
STEEL

What is metal?
All metal comes from rocks in the ground. Rock is broken up and heated to get the metal out.

When was metal discovered?
As far back as 11,000 years ago, early people were making tools and jewellery out of metal. Today we make things like watches, wire, and even spaceships!

How is foil made?
The foil wrap we use in cooking is made of ALUMINIUM, which comes from a rock called bauxite. To turn it into foil, a block of aluminium is squashed through rollers again and again until it's a long flat sheet.

Who invented the CAN?
A Frenchman, Nicholas Appert, invented the STEEL can in 1810 to preserve food for Napoleon's army.

Metal uses
So many things around you are made from metal or have metal in them. Look around your kitchen – cookers, saucepans, and cutlery are all made of metal. That's because it is strong and easy to clean.

Recycle metal
Every time you recycle metal you are saving the Earth from being dug up. Rock that contains metal can't grow back. Once it's dug up, that's it!

Test your metal
Hold a magnet near a pile of cans – you'll find some will stick. These are made of STEEL. **STEEL cans are 100% recyclable.** Most drinks cans are made of ALUMINIUM, which can be recycled and made into just about anything from cars to brand new cans, so RECYCLE!

Mysterious metal

Test your metal
Find out whether metals are magnetic by touching a magnet into onto various objects – if it sticks, they're magnetic.

Fishing game
Cut fish shapes out of paper and fasten a paper clip or paper fastener onto them. Tie a magnet onto a piece of string, tie the string to a pencil, then race your friends to pick up the fish.

Moving metal
Metals are attracted to magnets – that's the magic of metal – so dig out those magnets. Here's how to make metal work for you.

KNOW YOUR STUFF
STEEL is 100% recyclable and keeps its quality, so make sure it gets recycled.

Tidy tins
Tin cans are great to reuse as storage, and because they are metal, you can decorate them with magnets. You can even spell out what is in them with letter magnets.

! Ask an ADULT
to cut the top off the can. Make sure it's clean and free from sharp edges.

Home-made fridge magnets
Glue a magnet to the top of a jar or bottle lid, then glue a small toy to the other side. Stick your magnets onto tins or even the fridge door.

Reuse lids from jars.

Magnets

Strong glue

Small toys

Cover a lid with foil.

Make a moving picture

1.
Make a base by cutting out a piece of thin card – try using the back of a cereal packet.

Decorate the background.

2.

Cut out cat shapes from thin card.

Paper fastener

Cut out separate hands and feet.

3.
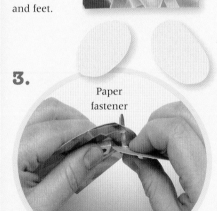

Paper fastener

Push a paper fastener through the face to make the cat's nose. Then push it through the body.

BACK OF PICTURE

Attach the cat to the card by pressing the paper fastener through the back of the card.

Crazy Cat – make him dance!

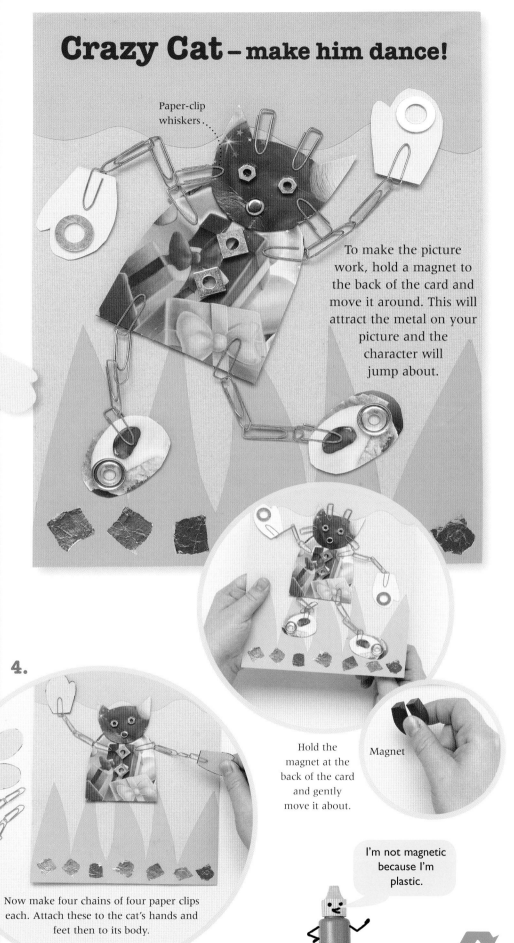

Paper-clip whiskers

Paper fastener

To make the picture work, hold a magnet to the back of the card and move it around. This will attract the metal on your picture and the character will jump about.

4.
Now make four chains of four paper clips each. Attach these to the cat's hands and feet then to its body.

Hold the magnet at the back of the card and gently move it about.

Magnet

I'm not magnetic because I'm plastic.

43

Metal Muddle

Shiny shapes.

Collect lots of shiny metal
objects and let them hang,
swing, and dangle.
Watch the
metal glisten
and sparkle.

Washers
and eyelets

Coiled wire from
a note book

Key

Safety-pin
chain

Foil dish

Foil sweet
wrapper

Hair
grip

Food bag ties have metal inside.

Chains

Old keys

Paper clips

Make a muddle

To make your metal dangle, take a wire coat hanger and pull it into a diamond shape. Fasten pieces of wire across the hanger – this makes a frame to hang your metal objects on. Attach some things onto the wire and hang others on chains of paperclips and safety pins.

Pull it into a diamond shape

Wire coat hanger

Use bag ties to fasten things in place.

Fasten pieces of wire across the coat hanger.

Paper fastener

Safety pins

Metal fork

Tie things to the frame

Use a paper clip as a hook

Small strainer

Any metal will work – see what you can find at home.

Wire from a notebook

Cookie cutter

Foil dishes

45

Make a mobile

Reuse clean foil dishes and decorate them with sweet wrappers and other shiny metal bits. Attach paperclips and chains to hang them up.

Glue foil sweet wrappers to the foil dishes.

Strong glue

All these trays are made of ALUMINIUM.

KNOW YOUR STUFF

Squash a sweet wrapper into a ball. If it's made of metal foil, it will stay in a ball.

Mirror mobiles

Reflect the light with these simple mobiles. Hang them in a sunny window to shimmer and shine.

Link paperclips together to make a chain.

Glue different-sized dishes together.

Link dishes together with a paperclip.

Pipe cleaners are made of metal too!

Metal models

Space age

Build metal robots, rockets, and aliens and create a shiny, lunar landscape.

.... Foil-dish hat

.... Foil-tube head

4.

Glue them together.

Make a model

Foil food trays are a good start for the robot body. Cut down cardboard tubes for the legs and head, and wrap them in kitchen foil. Then use bits and bobs for your metal man's features.

1.

Toilet or kitchen roll tubes can be covered in foil.

Wrap them up tightly.

.... Pipe-cleaner arms.

.... Use strong glue to attach his face and buttons.

2.

Tape the tube legs to the tray.

3.

Tape the arms onto the tray.

Space rocket

Tape a foil dish to the base...

Make a metal cone with shiny card, or by wrapping plain card in foil.

Wrap a drink can in foil. ....

Lunar landscape

Lay down lots of foil sweet wrappers to make a colourful lunar surface. Then build your own metal robots. Do they look like the ones on this page?

Metal washers ....

Pipe cleaners can be bent into all sorts of shapes. ...

Paper clips ....

KNOW YOUR STUFF
Recycling one aluminium can saves enough energy to run a TV for three hours.

Aha! Foiled again.

Fabric – it's what the clothes we wear are made of! It can be soft, furry, scratchy, strong, or stretchy. Yarns can be woven or knitted to make all kinds of garments.

Fabric

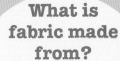

Imagine our world without fabric – we would probably catch a cold without clothes. Furniture is covered in fabric so it's soft and comfortable to sit on.

What is fabric made from?

WOOL comes from sheep, SILK from silk worms, COTTON from cotton plants, LINEN from flax plants. These are all natural products.

When was fabric invented?

The Egyptians first wove cotton into cloth about 14,000 years ago. The Romans built the first wool factory 1,500 years ago.

How is fabric made?

Fabric is usually woven from yarns like wool and cotton. Wool is sheared off the sheep (like a hair cut), then spun into woollen yarn. Yarn can be woven into fabric – see page 56 to try weaving for yourself.

Lycra, nylon, and polyester

Fabrics like these are called synthetic because they are man-made in laboratories. They are more like plastics than fabric.

How your fabric can help others

Take the clothes you've grown out of to charity shops. They will not only be used by someone else but they will make money for charity too.

Look out for labels

Many clothes and other fabrics can be reused or recycled. Look at the labels – this one tells you the fabric is wool.

Recycling fabric

Remake clothes and fabric into something else. See the projects in this section for some good ideas. If the fabric is falling apart, it can be made into filling for mattresses and insulation. So recycle your old towels, bed sheets, table linen, and curtains.

Making friends

They're woolly, they're soft, they're your bobble-hat and glove friends! Have you grown out of your woolly warmers? Then transform them into cuddly creatures.

KNOW YOUR STUFF
Jumpers and other items made of wool can be respun – the fibres are used again, to make new clothes.

How to make woolly friends

Take a glove and decide what shape you want it to be. Turn to page 54 to find out how to do back stitch, which will help you when you sew up the fingers.

1.

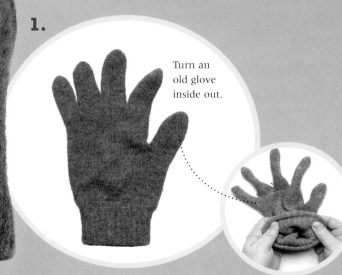

Turn an old glove inside out.

Make new friends from old

All kinds of gloves can be used – from baby mittens to Dad's big gloves. Experiment with how many fingers to use.

Try stuffing your old hats to make us!

I'm a glove with short fingers.

I've got a thumb nose.

......Use all the fingers to make my hair.

2.

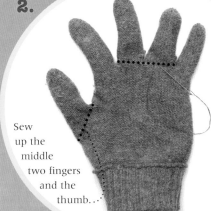

Sew up the middle two fingers and the thumb...

Turn the glove right side out again.

Push out the fingers that haven't been sewn up.

Cotton wool and old tights are great for stuffing gloves......

3.

Now make a face using stitches, fabric scraps, or buttons.

Stuff the glove.

Sew up the bottom.

Hold onto your hats!

Don't chuck them, recycle them.

Ask your family to give you their old hats. The more you have, the more bobble-hat people you can make.

This bow came from a hat............

Put a bow on your hat and make me – Betty Bow

A quick sewing lesson

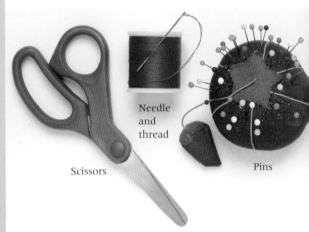

Scissors

Needle and thread

Pins

Back stitch

Back stitch is a good stitch to use because it keeps the stuffing in well. Practise on a piece of material before you start.

Knot the end of the thread and push the needle down and up through the fabric.

Pull the needle all the way through to the knot.

Now push the needle half way between the knot and the dangling thread.

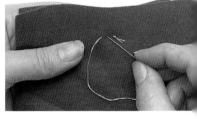

Bring the needle up in front of the dangling cotton.

Repeat these steps and sew over the last stitch to finish off.

KNOW YOUR STUFF

Over 70% of the world's population uses second-hand clothes.

What to use for stuffing

You can use almost any soft fabric for stuffing. Old socks and tights are probably the pieces of clothing people throw away most often, so gather them up before they go!

How to make Bob Bobble

Try to find two hats that are about the same size. Ideally, Bob should have one hat without a bobble, and one hat with a bobble. But you can always make your own pom-pom to go on top.

..........Find two hats, about the same size.

Sew on buttons or fabric scraps to make Bob Bobble's face.

Old buttons

6. Now make the face

1. Pin the hats together

..........Turn the top hat upside down.

..........Turn the bottom hat inside out.

Place the top hat into the bottom hat...

..........Pin the edges together.

Sew up the opening neatly.

5. Sew up the gap

2. Sew the hats together

Sew along the pins, leaving a 12 cm (5 in) opening at the end...

Keep stuffing until Bob feels really full.

4. Stuff

Turn the hats right-side-out through the opening...

Push your stuffing through the opening.

3. Turn right-side-out

Rag mats

Revive old rags

Collect up material and old clothes, cut them into strips, and weave them into pretty mats.

To make strips longer, knot them together.

Cut long strips of cloth 2 cm (1 in) wide.

Cutting the strips

Cut the material into long strips. Use one colour for the main weave that goes up and down, called the "warp", and lots of colours and fabrics for the "weft" – the material the goes across.

Use any old fabric.

How to start

Use a cardboard sheet for your weaving frame. Cut an even number of slits at the top and bottom. Knot together lots of the same colour strips to make one very long strip.

12 slits ......

...... Cut the slits 1 cm (½ in) apart.

Cardboard sheet 20 x 30 cm (8 x 12 in)

12 slits ......

Slip the fabric into the first slit.

Thread the fabric through each slit in turn, around and around from front to back.

Weaving the weft

Weave the strips over and under the main colour – the warp. Pull the strip all the way through before starting the next line. Leave a bit at the beginning and weave it back on itself to anchor it.

When you reach the end, turn the strip around and go back again.

Weave in the other direction, tucking under where you went over.

Knot a new fabric strip onto the end and carry on weaving.

Continue weaving – don't do it too tight.

Weave the last colour and secure the end by weaving it back on itself.

Finishing off

Turn the board over.

Cut through the fabric strips.

Gently pull the fabric strips through the slits.

Knot pairs of strips together.

Trim them to the same length.

Pocket purses

Don't chuck your old clothes – they might provide perfect pocket purses!

I'm just right for your pocket money!

How to make a purse

Search out an old piece of clothing with a pocket on the outside – one with a zip or button is ideal. Cut around the pocket with pinking shears (scissors with zig-zag edges) and you have your pocket purse – it's as easy as that!

Pinking shears prevent the edges from fraying.

Pinking shears

Trouser bags
Rescue your favourite old jeans and turn them into these cool bags.

KNOW YOUR STUFF
Even when fabric is so worn out it's falling to bits, it's still worth recycling. It can be used for insulation and filling for mattresses.

Recycle your trousers and skirts,

make glam bags for school,

and purses to pop in the pockets.

Fabric

How to make a glam bag

Recycle old trousers

to make these glamorous bags. Simply cut off the legs, sew up the opening, and attach a handle.

Needle, cotton and pins

1.

Cut off the trouser tops just above the legs.

2.

Turn inside out.

Turn the top inside out and pin the two bottom edges together.

Stitch.

3. Turn right way out.

Use pinking shears so the material won't fray.

Add a strap

Use the material from one leg to make your strap. Cut a length about 3 cm (1 in) wide and sew it in place.

Pin the strap in place.

Sew it tightly.

Glam it up

When you have finished
your bag, decorate it with
beads, badges, and bows.
Then there are all those
handy pockets to fill!

Make a matching
pocket purse....

Fancy strap

You could use a
ribbon for the strap,
like this pink
velvet one.

Comfy cushions

Snuggle up to your favourite T-shirt or jeans after you have grown out of them. Brighten up your bedroom with these quirky cushions.

Clothing cushions

As well as reusing your T-shirts, try making Glam bags (page 60-61) into cushions too.

The pockets are still handy.

These look cosy – now you can enjoy your favourite clothes for longer!

KNOW YOUR STUFF

Most discarded clothes are still in good condition. DON'T BURY THEM IN A LANDFILL – give them to charity instead.